D0561063

LET THERE BE LIGHT

LET THERE

BE LIGHT

poems by

PHILIP APPLEMAN

Harper Perennial
A Division of HarperCollins*Publishers*

FIRST EDITION

Designed by Cassandra J. Pappas

Library of Congress Cataloging-in-Publication Data

Appleman, Philip, 1926–
    Let there be light : poems / by Philip Appleman.
      p. cm.
    ISBN 0-06-055273-5 (cloth)—ISBN 0-06-096832-X (pbk.)
    I. Title.
  PS3551.P6L48   1991
  811'.54—dc20   90–55488

---

91 92 93 94 95 CG/MPC 10 9 8 7 6 5 4 3 2 1
91 92 93 94 95 CG/MPC 10 9 8 7 6 5 4 3 2 1 (pbk.)

In memory of Gertrude and Martha,
my two mothers,
who always understood

and

for Margie,
the poetry in my life,
who shared this journey
and helped make the book

CONTENTS

Acknowledgments   *ix*

I. THE BIBLE RETOLD FOR GROWNUPS   1

Gathering at the River   3

Eve   5

An Eye for an Eye   7

Heavenly Body   8

Sarah   11

Sensual Music   19

Our Tree   20

Bildad   21

Gertrude   26

Anniversary   28

The Trickle-Down Theory of Happiness   30

Last-Minute Message for a Time Capsule   31

II. INTO THE WIND   33

New Year's Day   35

David   36

Night Thoughts   39

Desire   40

Noah   41

Watching Her Sleep   51

Another Word for Jim   52

Life on the Mississippi Queen   53

Fleas   54

Jonah   56

Gifts   59

Before You Push the Red Button   61

III. THE TREE OF KNOWLEDGE   63

And Then the Perfect Truth of Hatred   65

Mary   67

Credo   70

Coast to Coast   72

Judas   73

Thin Ice   75

Heading North   76

Martha   77

Lighting Your Birthday Cake   79

Jesus   80

But the Daisies Will Not Be Deceived by the Gods   82

ACKNOWLEDGMENTS

Grateful acknowledgment is made to the following publications, in which some of the poems first appeared; several of them have been revised or retitled for this book.

Amicus Journal: "Last-Minute Message for a Time Capsule"
Beloit Poetry Journal: "Judas"
Bluefish: "Another Word for Jim"
College English: "Fleas"
Confrontation: "Eve"
Intervention: "Before You Push the Red Button"
Kentucky Poetry Review: "But the Daisies Will Not Be Deceived by
    the Gods," "Desire," "Martha"; *Special Philip Appleman
    Issue, Spring 1989:* "Bildad," "Credo," "Gifts," "Lighting
    Your Birthday Cake," "Mary," "Our Tree," "Sarah"
Long Island Quarterly: "New Year's Day"
The Nation: "Life on the Mississippi Queen"
North Atlantic Review: "Jonah"
Partisan Review: "Gertrude," "Jesus," "Watching Her Sleep"
Pivot: "And Then the Perfect Truth of Hatred," "Thin Ice"
Poetry: "Anniversary," "An Eye for an Eye," "Gathering at the
    River," "Heading North," "Heavenly Body," "Sensual
    Music," "The Trickle-Down Theory of Happiness"
Under Open Sky: Poets on William Cullen Bryant: "Night Thoughts"

A version of "Noah" was the title poem of *Darwin's Ark* (Indiana
University Press, 1984).

I

THE BIBLE RETOLD
FOR GROWNUPS

GATHERING AT THE RIVER ⌁

Is it
crossing over Jordan
to a city of light, archangels
ceaselessly trumpeting over
the heavenly choirs: perpetual Vivaldi,
jasper and endless topaz and amethyst,
the Sistine ceiling seven days a week,
the everlasting smirk
of perfection?

Is it
the river Styx,
darkness made visible, fire
that never stops: endless murder
too merciless to kill,
massacres on an endless loop,
the same old victims always
coming back for more?

Or is it the silky muck
of Wabash and Maumee, the skirr
and skim of blackbirds,
fields of Queen Anne's lace
and bumblebees? Well,
go out once more, and feel
the crumble of dry loam,
fingers and soil slowly becoming
the same truth: there in the hand
is our kinship with oak, our bloodline
to cattle. Imagine,

not eons of boredom or pain,
but honest earth-to-earth;
and when our bodies rise again,
they will be wildflowers, then rabbits,
then wolves, singing a perfect love
to the beautiful, meaningless moon.

EVE 〜

Clever, he was, so slick
he could weave words into sunshine.
When he murmured another refrain
of that shimmering promise, "You
shall be as gods," something with wings
whispered back in my heart,
and I crunched the apple—a taste so good
I just had to share it with Adam,
and all of a sudden
we were naked.
Oh, yes, we were nude before, but now,
grabbing for fig leaves, we knew
that we knew too much, just as the slippery
serpent said—so we crouched all day
under the rhododendrons, trembling
at something bleak and windswept in our bellies
that soon we'd learn to call by its right name:
fear.
God was furious with the snake
and hacked off his legs, on the spot.
And for us
it was thorns and thistles,
sweat of the brow, dust
to dust returning. In that sizzling
skyful of spite whirled
the whole black storm of the future:
the flint knife in Abel's heart,
the incest that swelled us into a tribe,
a nation, and
brought us all, like driven lambs,

straight to His flood.
I blamed it on human nature, even then,
when there were only two humans around,
and if human nature was a mistake,
whose mistake was it? *I* didn't ask
to be cursed with curiosity, I only wanted
the apple,
and of course that promise—to be
like gods. But then,
maybe we are like gods.
Maybe we're all exactly like gods.
And maybe that's our really original
sin.

AN EYE FOR AN EYE 〜

Are you saved?'' he asks me,
sunrise in the corner of his eye,
a snag at the edge of his voice.
In a blur of memory, I see the others:
the preacher who used to trounce my tender sins,
kids at church camp, their brimstone choirs
shrill with teenage lust gone underground,
true believers come knocking to tell me
that flaming hell is real.
And those twisted faces on the tube:
Christian gunmen in Beirut, their hot eyes
exploding in the beds of sleeping children;
the righteous hatreds of Belfast, lighting
Irish eyes like a tenement fire;
the eyes of the Ayatollah, squinting with joy
at the blood of his blindfolded prisoners.
It smolders in the windows of the soul,
that holy blaze, never so bright
as in human sacrifice,
never so proud as in crimson crusades,
the glorious, godlike destruction.

HEAVENLY BODY ~

Halley's Comet, 1985, 1986

1

　　　"Comet," from the Greek, means
　　　a curve
　　　of golden hair.
Plotting the curves:
parabolas of calf,
ellipses of thigh, and
little worlds adrift
in mystery—
what is the secret name
for the bend inside the knee,
and what is the word
for the arc between
the first and second toe?
　　　　Springtime:
　　　　out there on the sand
　　　　horseshoe crabs are clattering
　　　　their armor-plated love—
　　　　everything that matters
　　　　will return.

2

　　　In our dark ages, comets burn
　　　their warnings in the sky,
　　　famines, plagues, the death of kings—

          or nothing in our lives
          except our lives.
Massaging her back: a love song
played along a xylophone of spine,
feeling out the valleys of her nape,
the graceful curve of shoulder—but
what do we call
that little tuck behind the shoulder blades,
and what is the word for the tempting
dimples in her loins?
          Autumn:
          a million monarchs
          fly their royal destiny
          across the continent, returning
          again, and yet again
          for love.

3

          "Perihelion" is also Greek, meaning
          the closest we can get, our inner
          outer limit, the strongest pull of all
          our gravity.
Deep inside her, everything
is silk and velvet, spring
and fall, rhythms in
the memory of hips—but
what is the word
for that sudden tightness in the throat,
and what do we call
the craving in the heart

just before the murky sky
showers a thousand stars across our bed?
Spring: mayflies brood upon
the tragedy of evening and
the grand design of their
return.
Fall: the golden-haired traveler reappears,
shining toward perihelion,
and vermilion floats
from the fingers of maple trees
to mulch again our secret words
for love.

SARAH

You remember me,
the tough-luck wife of Abraham—
a beauty, they called me
in the old days in Egypt, a flower
fit for Pharaohs. But now
I'm just a gray granny who pesters you
with the tales they used to tell
around the evening fire . . .

The story goes
that after the great flood drained away—
drained away to *where*, I always wondered—
then Noah came limping down the gangplank,
feeling older than old, downright ante-
diluvian, and looked around, left and right.
Everywhere he looked
he saw nothing with those cloudy eyes
but landscapes of corpses and skeletons.
So who could blame him if he drank too much
and sprawled around in the buff all day? I mean,
given that heavy load of guilt,
friends and neighbors gone to mushy death,
wouldn't you?
Anyway, that's all the poor guy did
for over three hundred years until,
just twenty candles shy of Methuselah's record,
he finally turned up his toes.
Meanwhile Shem, Ham, and Japheth
and their anonymous wives were going at it
day and night, getting the begetting going
again, the way the Lord commanded. Sure enough,

Shem—a hundred years old after the flood—
Shem begat a son he named
Arphaxad.
In due time
Arphaxad begat Salah
who begat Eber
who begat Peleg—
and so it went, for another hundred years,
until Terah begat my husband, Abram,
and Abram's brother, the father of Lot.

When he came to itchy manhood, Abram
looked upon me with favor—I
was an eyeful in those days, remember—and
he made me his wife.
We all moved off to Canaan,
Abram in the country to the west, Lot near a more
sophisticated town called Sodom.
And we prospered.
But then
God changed Abram's name to Abraham,
and told him, "Look, I've heard
that Sodom over there is a swamp of perversion,
Gomorrah, too. If that's really true . . ."

We both knew God well enough to see
where this was heading.
We still remembered the flood, not
that long ago, after all.
We knew that when God
gets into a rage, He smites

everything in sight, rain falling
on the just and the unjust. Then
Abraham thought of his nephew Lot,
doing so well with his flocks and herds
over by Sodom,
so before God gets ten steps away,
he runs after Him, shouting,
"Lord! Lord! Wait a minute! How about
all the *good* folks over there? Family men,
chaste women, keepers of the Sabbath,
salt of the earth—
are you going to blast them right along
with the perverts? Listen,
there might be, say, fifty saints
in that poor town.
Wouldn't you save it, for their sakes?"
Oh, that was nervy enough, but then
I thought I'd collapse
when Abraham turns the screw again:
"Shall not . . ." he begins—I can see his legs
quivering as he says it—"Shall not
the Judge of all the earth
do right?"

When I dare to look,
they're still nose to nose,
my poor Abe quaking like a weed in a windstorm,
but firm in his nephew's cause,
and God, gone white as a thunderhead, but so far
not losing His temper the way He always did
down in Egypt, blazing away

at everything that moved.
Pretty soon He nods a bit,
like a camel trader who's just been outwitted,
and mutters, "All right, Abraham,
you find me fifty diamonds
in that dirt, and I'll back off."
He turns to go, and finally
I can breathe again. But then
Abraham calls out,
"God! Yahweh! Listen! I'm a nothing,
I'm the dirt under your sandals,
I'm the ashes from your campfire,
I'm a pest, forgive me for asking,
I shouldn't mention it—but suppose,
just suppose I come up short by five, just five short,
what then, would you burn the place for five?"
God is a little quicker this time—
you know how it is, once you have
a deal cooking, things go easier—
and He says, gritting His teeth a little,
"All right, Abraham, Patriarch,
Father of My Nation, for forty-five
I'll save the slimy place."
But before I can relax,
Abe blurts out, not even pretending
to grovel, "How about forty?"
God comes right back,
"OK, forty,
forty's OK,"

…e a nervous tic, irresistible, his voice
…ll of the fever of wheeling and dealing, and of course
…e unbearable fear of losing it all—
…ter so many years I recognize
…e symptoms. *"God!"* he shouts.
…y stomach cramps up, my eyes squeeze shut,
…aiting for the end. "God,
…on't get mad, I swear
…is is the last time,
…ut wait—*how about ten?"*
…nd I catch the quick crackle of lightning,
…e stench of burning flesh . . .
…ut no, it's only God's voice,
…ding in the distance: "I will not
…estroy it for ten's sake."

…o that, at last, is that. Abraham
…s still standing there in our gravel path,
…weat staining his summer robes.
…run to him and hug him, glad
…or the little cakes I baked for God that morning,
…lad for the fatted calf we killed
…nd fed Him, knowing that full bellies
…ake good tempers. But Abe is all unstrung
…y the terrible chance he's taken.
…s I lead him back to the tent like a cripple,
…e mumbles again and again, how hard it is
…o make the Judge of all the earth
…o right.

…ou can guess what happened next.

and turns on His heel.

So this time when Abraham calls again, I figure
it's all up with us, he's gone too far,
you can't haggle like this, not
with the Lord Himself, not even
in the Middle East. But Abraham
goes all oily: "God, please, don't get mad,
but say now—how about thirty?"
God doesn't even turn around. "Thirty. Done."
And Abe: "Twenty? Twenty righteous souls,
twenty virtuous, circumcised, ram-killing,
bullock-burning, tithe-paying citizens
who love the Lord?"
God is slouching down our front path,
kicking stones. I can barely hear
His gruff voice: "All right. Agreed.
It's a deal."

And I pray to myself—quit
while you're still ahead, Abraham! This
is the Lord of flood and plague,
the jealous God, God of the flaming sword,
the God of pestilence, the Angel of Death,
you're playing with fire, enough, enough!

But he has to do it one more time,
old goat-seller, bargain-hunter,
carpet-buyer, his whole life an endless
flea market, it must have come over him

There hadn't even been a handshake,
let alone a contract, and like they say
out here in the Holy Land, a verbal deal
isn't worth the parchment it's written on.
So to make a long story short,
when Lot heard that God was reneging,
he got out of Sodom fast,
taking his wife and daughters
up to the mountains, an angel warning them
not to look back on that holy
holocaust. But when the red-hot coals
winged over Sodom, and the fire
began falling from heaven, Lot's wife
just *had* to check it out, just for a minute. And God,
with that sense of humor He's famous for,
turned her into a pillar of salt, ha-ha.
Then Lot and his two sexy daughters
dug into a cave, where they all got drunk,
and there, in the godly stink of brimstone, enjoyed
a little incest, and the two girls
both gave birth to sons. Or brothers, depending
on how you look at it. And Lot had sons,
or grandsons, suit yourself, and that's
all I'm going to say about that family. I mean,
if you put this in a book,
nobody in his right mind would believe it.

But whenever I think of Sodom . . . Well,
what had those people done that was so bad,
anyway—some dice and booze,

some frisky girls, willing boys,
a little fooling around—I know
it's not exactly orthodox, but
to kill them all? To peel
the cooked flesh off those one-year-olds,
just learning their first words?
All I can say is,
God must have a weird sense of values,
and if there's a Judgment Day,
as some folks think,
He's going to have a lot to answer for.

BILDAD ~

I know what they're saying
under their breath, behind my back,
men in the sweaty bazaar,
women at the well near sundown. "He's
a tent flap in the wind," they're saying.
"His knots have come loose. Bildad
can't walk and count goats at the same time."
Well, let them talk. We knew
what we were doing, Zophar,
Eliphaz, and I, we knew our minds,
our duty, our holy obligation.
So we sat with Job for seven days
and seven nights, for his own good.
What, after all,
was in it for us but righteousness,
piety, the love of God—a God as good
and kind and loving and just
as we were?

Job was our friend, so when we heard
how his thousands of sheep and camels and oxen
were carried off, his children slaughtered,
servants put to the sword,
his body blistered with boils,
and only his wife still alive
to scald him with her constant
"Curse God and die"—
why naturally we had to come and sit with him,
there in the ashes. He was a mess,
frankly—those festering sores,
his head shaved ragged, his robe in tatters,

and he smelled like a day-old fish—
but what's all that among friends?

We wanted to let him talk first,
so we waited. And waited.
After those seven long days he finally spoke:
"God breaks me like a tempest.
He wounds me without cause."

That's when our sacred mission began:
"Job, you've got it all wrong,
God doesn't punish the innocent.
Think, deep in your heart,
where you've sinned, but don't
blame the Lord."
That shook him up, his eyes
darting around at us like someone
looking for a way to run.
"But I *am* innocent!" he whined.
We all had to smile,
and he jabbered on, "The arrows of the Almighty
are poisoning me. Let the day perish
when I was born . . ."
We shut him off, before his self-pity
stuck to our skin like pitch.
"Job! A hypocrite's hope
is a spiderweb, a flower in the withering sun,
its roots in stone—but the good Lord
will not cast away a perfect man."

Oh, we had him all right,

locked in logic.
He twisted and turned, and hassled us
with more of his graveyard metaphor:
"Man that is born of woman," he wailed,
"cometh forth like a flower
and is cut down. Man dieth
and riseth not. If God's scourge
kills the innocent, He
will sit there and laugh . . ."

We stopped him short. "Job,
the light of the wicked
shall be put out, the hypocrite ·
perish, the meat in his bowels
turned to gall, he shall vomit up
his ill-gotten riches,
he shall suck the poison of asps, burn
fire in his private places. So
confess—you must have stripped
the naked of their clothing,
sent widows away empty-handed, broken
the arms of orphans. Almighty God
is just. Confess. *Confess.*"

I tell you we had him. Our syllogism
was airtight: since God is just,
He cannot torment
an innocent man;
the conclusion was as clear

as a desert sky. Job
must be guilty.

But then God opened His mouth
and in a whirlwind of rage
blasted our beautiful logic.
Out of a dust storm it came, that booming
irrelevance: "Where were you
when I made the earth, the stars,
the sea? Do you know the breadth of the world,
the treasures of the snow?
Out of whose womb comes the ice?
Can you send down the lightning?"
And more of the same, all meaning—
Why do you bother Me with your sniveling,
you insignificant maggot?
"Will you condemn Me," roared
the grimy whirlwind, "so you can be righteous?"

Some scene, isn't it? There we are,
making sense of things, putting Job in his place,
proving the neat connection between
crime and punishment—and just as our triumph
burns in Job's bewildered eyes,
God horns in with that scandalous
non sequitur. "No," He says,
"You don't suffer because you sin.
You suffer because I say so."

And Job, humble at last in spirit
as he already was in body, groveled in dirt:

"I abhor myself Lord—I repent
in dust and ashes."

That did it. God
was finally satisfied, and Job
got his reward: his camels back,
doubled, his sheep and oxen, too, and now
his wife is pregnant, a brand-new bundle
on its way. As I always say,
toadying is good for business. Still,
this whole affair
was just cosmic whimsy, and
who needs it? That's why I don't care
when the locals whisper behind my back
and call me crazy.

But I've got children, too. Who's
going to explain this
celestial farce
to them? All I can hope now is
that Job will be utterly forgotten, and
that God's awful pronouncement
will be buried in Job's grave.
It's hard enough to bring up a family
in these troubled times without admitting
that almighty God has the morals
of a Babylonian butcher.

GERTRUDE 〜

(Gertrude Appleman, 1901–1976)

> *God is all-knowing, all-present, and almighty.*
> —A Catechism of Christian Doctrine

I wish that all the people
who peddle God
could watch my mother die:
could see the skin and
gristle weighing in
at seventy-nine, every stubborn
pound of flesh a small
death.

I wish the people who peddle God
could see her young,
lovely in gardens and
beautiful in kitchens, and could watch
the hand of God slowly
twisting her knees and fingers
till they gnarled and knotted, settling in
for thirty years of pain.

I wish the people who peddle God
could see the lightning
of His cancer stabbing
her, that small frame
tensing at every shock,
her sweet contralto scratchy with
the Lord's infection: *Philip,*
I want to die.

I wish I had them gathered round,
those preachers, popes, rabbis,
imams, priests—every
pious shill on God's payroll—and I
would pull the sheets from my mother's brittle body,
and they would fall on their knees at her bedside
to be forgiven all their
faith.

ANNIVERSARY ⌇

Maybe it wasn't strange to find
drums and cymbals where
there might have been violins, maybe
we couldn't have known; besides,
would it have mattered?
See what the years have left behind:
a thick scar in the palm of my hand,
a ragged one running along the arm.
And you:
I know your scars at midnight
by touch.

Everything we've learned, we've picked up
by ear, a pidgin language
of the heart, just
enough to get by on:
we know the value of cacophony, how to measure
with a broken yardstick,
what to do with bruised fruit.
Reading torn maps, we always
make it home, riding
on empty.

And whatever this is we've built together,
we remember sighting it skew, making it plumb
eventually, and here it stands,
stone over rock. In the walls
there are secret passages
leading to music nobody else can hear,
earthlight nobody else can see. And somewhere

in a room that's not yet finished
there are volumes in our own hand, telling
troubled tales, promises kept, and
promises
still to keep.

THE TRICKLE-DOWN THEORY OF HAPPINESS ~

Out of heaven, to bless the high places,
it falls on the penthouses, drizzling
at first, then a pelting allegro,
and Dick and Jane skip to the terrace
and go boogieing through the azaleas,
while mommy and daddy come running
with pots and pans, glasses, and basins
and try to hold all of it up there,
but no use, it's too much, it keeps coming,
and pours off the edges, down limestone
to the pitchers and pails on the ground, where
delirious residents catch it,
and bucket brigades get it moving
inside, until bathtubs are brimful,
but still it keeps coming, that shower
of silver in alleys and gutters,
all pouring downhill to the sleazy
red brick, and the barefoot people
who romp in it, laughing, but never
take thought for tomorrow, all spinning
in a pleasure they catch for a moment;
so when Providence turns off the spigot
and the sky goes as dry as a prairie,
then daddy looks down from the penthouse,
down to the streets, to the gutters,
and his heart goes out to his neighbors,
to the little folk thirsty for laughter,
and he prays in his boundless compassion:
on behalf of the world and its people
he demands of his God, *give me more.*

LAST-MINUTE MESSAGE FOR A TIME CAPSULE

I have to tell you this, whoever you are:
that on one summer morning here, the ocean
pounded in on tumbledown breakers,
a south wind, bustling along the shore,
whipped the froth into little rainbows,
and a reckless gull swept down the beach
as if to fly were everything it needed.
I thought of your hovering saucers,
looking for clues, and I wanted to write this down,
so it wouldn't be lost forever—
that once upon a time we had
meadows here, and astonishing things,
swans and frogs and luna moths
and blue skies that could stagger your heart.
We could have had them still,
and welcomed you to earth, but
we also had the righteous ones
who worshipped the True Faith, and Holy War.
When you go home to your shining galaxy,
say that what you learned
from this dead and barren place is
to beware the righteous ones.

II

INTO THE WIND

NEW YEAR'S DAY ~

grabs you and yanks you forward: this
is no seduction, this is the rape
of tomorrow, next week, the blind thrust
up there ahead in the haze that is
the future, waiting
for one false move, one shiver
of desperate hope—then
the crystal dome shatters, and a random shard
trashes your dreams like a thug.
Now, before another minute
grips you by the shirt, now
is the time to count your mixed
blessings: that you get older and older
and older, every brawl
beefing up brawn, every fracture healing
to flint. So
you lob your resolution into the clouds—
you will take each sleet storm as it comes,
face into the wind, slog
through endless mud, and kick away one
disaster at a time. Every hour
your skin will be tougher, your eyesight
clearer, and on that final day, when
you have made the dazzling discovery,
you will call back joy to everyone:
all is well, all is well,
we are alone.

DAVID ⁓

After my smooth stone crushed
his head, I hacked at the throat
with his own great sword
and dragged back my ugly trophy,
oozing blood. Then
came the rout and the sexy slaughter—
I gave the guts of Philistine boys
to the buzzards and beasts
of the earth. Our women
sang in the streets, "O Saul
has slain his thousands, but David
his tens of thousands."
   I am David, I am mighty,
    and behold, the Lord is with me.

For my promised wife Michal, King Saul
demanded the foreskins of
one hundred Gentiles. I made instead
two hundred weeping widows
and cast those gory flaps
at the feet of the king, amid praises.
And God said, "I will deliver all
the Philistines into thy hands."
So I smote them hip and thigh,
and we spitted every man,
and buried our tools and our knives
in the soft flesh of their women, blood
sticky under our feet, the skulls of their children
smashed in our holy crusade.

No one escaped the justice of our God.
   I am David, I am mighty,
   and behold, the Lord is with me.

I took Michal, daughter of Saul,
to be my wife and lover;
I took Abigail, a widow,
to be my wife and lover;
and then Ahinoam
to be my wife and lover;
then Maacah and Abital
and Haggith and Eglah,
to be my wives and lovers—
and concubines without number.
But when I saw Bathsheba, no one
could satisfy me till I had her.
So, being king, I had her,
and murdered her faithful husband. When
the Lord carried off my baby boy,
our gloomy local prophet
said unto me, "Thou art David,
and God hath put away
thy sin." In a tumult
of joy I smashed and burned
the ancient city of Rabbah
and made slaves and concubines
of all its godless people

who live without the blessings
of the Law.
    I am David, I am mighty,
    and behold, the Lord is with me.

Now the waves of death are upon me,
and I call upon the Lord:
the foundations of heaven move,
and smoke streams from His nostrils.
He thunders from the heavens
and rewards me much, according
to my righteousness, for
I have kept the laws of God.
He hath made all my ways to be perfect.
    I am David, I was mighty,
    and behold, the Lord is with me.

NIGHT THOUGHTS ～

Black on black, from Maine to California:
the starshine is too precious now to keep.
I'm staking all my luck on one more morning
while everyone I love is sound asleep.

Suppose tomorrow were the last clear dawning,
painting the sky with glimmers of desire,
the last pale cloud, the last bright eagle soaring,
before the final blossoming of fire—

the last green pine, and one more blue wave breaking,
the long farewell in one last robin's song,
teaching us the keenest kind of aching,
to love that well which we must leave 'ere long.

They'd feel it come in Washington and China:
the poison rain, the murder in the snow,
endless winter, birdless and benighted,
and sickness in the fields, where nothing grows.

From Paumanok it's black to the Pacific:
a nightbird says too late, you're in too deep.
Red telephones are jangling their dark traffic,
while everyone I love is sound asleep.

DESIRE 〜

1

The body
tugged like a tide, a pull
stronger than
the attraction of stars.

2

Moons
circling their planets,
planets
rounding their suns.

3

Nothing is what
we cannot imagine:
all that we know we know
moves in the muscles.

4

Undertow:
I reach for you,
oceans away.

NOAH ～

Seed of Methuselah,
already six hundred years old,
more than a little weary
from all that virtuous living—then
a finger out of the clouds pokes down at him,
and a Voice full of blood and bones
bullies the stony hillsides:
"Make thee an ark of gopher wood . . ."
Details follow, in that same
bossy baritone: "The boat shall be
four hundred fifty feet long
seventy-five feet wide
three decks
one window
one door."

And then
the Voice tells him why.

His sons, Shem, Ham, and Japheth, just
cannot handle this news.
"He's going to drown them all?" Japheth whispers,
"Every last woman and child? What for?"
Noah's mind is not what it used to be; lately
it strays like a lost lamb, his ancient voice
a bleat: "Ahh—
wickedness, I think that's
what He said—yes, wickedness."
Too vague for Japheth: "But wicked how? I mean,
what are the charges?"
The old brow wrinkles again. "Evil, that's

what He said. Corruption. Violence.''
''Violence! What do you call
this killer flood? He's going to murder
the lot of them, just
for making a few mistakes? For being—human?''
Now Japheth is really riled. Being the youngest,
he still has a lot of drinking pals around—
Enos and Jared, and sexy Adah
and his pretty young neighbor,
Zillah—together they'd put away
many a goatskin of red wine
under the big desert stars. Besides,
being a kid, a mere ninety years old,
he still likes to stump his father
with embarrassing questions. ''Listen,
Dad, I thought you said He
was omniscient—well, then,
wouldn't He have foreseen all this? And if He did,
why did He make us the way we are
in the first place?''

''Ours not to reason why,'' says Shem, the firstborn
and something of a prig. ''Ours but to build the ark.''
''That's another thing,'' Japheth scowls. ''Just
what *is* an ark? I mean,
we're desert people, after all—nomads,
living out here in this miserable dry scrub
with our smelly goats and camels—
I never saw a boat in my life.''
''I saw one once,'' Noah quavers,
''but I don't remember it very well,

that was four hundred years ago—
or was it five, let's see . . ."
"It can't be that hard," says Ham,
always the practical one. "An ordinary boat,
we'll mock one up. You need a keel, that's it,
you begin with a keel of gopher wood,
and the rest is easy—ribs, then planks,
pitch, decking. Don't worry, Dad,
I'll handle it."

So finally they have themselves an ark,
and God says, "Good work, Noah, now
get the animals—clean beasts, seven of a kind,
unclean, just two, but make sure
they're male and female, you got that straight?
And hurry it up, so I can get
the drowning started."
Noah was hoping the animals
would be easy, but Japheth
knows better. "Dad,
did He say *every* animal?"
"Every animal," Noah repeats,
quoting Authority. "Every living thing
of all flesh—fowl,
cattle, creeping things. Plus
food enough for a year."

Think of it—they're living out there
in that gritty wilderness, and all of a sudden
they're supposed to come up with two elephants.
Or is it more?

"Shem," Japheth calls. "Is the elephant
a clean or an unclean animal?
If it's clean, that means seven of them
and the ark is in trouble. And how
about rhinos? And hippos? What do we do
about the dinosaurs? How do we get a brontosaurus
up the gangplank?" Japheth
loves raising problems that Noah
hasn't thought of at all. "Pandas—kids
love pandas, we can't let them die out,
but how do we get two of them here
in a hurry, all the way from China?
And, oh, by the way, Dad,
how are we going to keep the lions
away from the lambs?"

It's not just a headache; it's a nightmare.
Just think of poor Ham, after all of his angst
and sweat getting the ark assembled, and then
having to trudge off to the Congo and the Amazon
to round up all those tricky
long-tailed leapers, there in the jungle greenery—
gibbons, orangutans, gorillas, baboons, chimps,
howler monkeys, spider monkeys, squirrel monkeys,
capuchins, mandrills, tamarins . . .

And Shem, dutiful Shem, in charge
of the other mammals—the giraffes,
the horses, zebras, quaggas, tapirs, bison,
the pumas, bears, shrews, raccoons, weasels,
skunks, mink, badgers, otters, hyenas,

the rats, bats, rabbits, chipmunks, beavers—
thousands of species of mammals . . .

And Japheth out there on the cliffs and treetops
trying to snare the birds—the eagles,
condors, hawks, buzzards, vultures, and every
winged beauty in the rain forests—and bring them back,
chattering, twittering, fluttering around
on the top deck, thousands upon thousands
of hyperkinetic birds . . .

Two by two
they come strolling through:
antelope, buffalo, camel, dog,
egret, ferret, gopher, frog,
quail and wombat, sheep and goose,
turtle, nuthatch, ostrich, moose,
ibex, jackal, kiwi, lark,
two by two they board the ark.

Well, it's pretty clear, isn't it,
that there's a space problem here: a boat
only four hundred fifty feet long, already
buzzing and bleating and squeaking and mooing
and grunting and mewing and hissing and cooing
and croaking and roaring and peeping and howling
and chirping and snarling and clucking and growling—
and the crocodiles aren't back from the Nile
yet, or the iguanas from the islands,
or the kangaroos or koalas, or
the pythons or boas or cotton-mouth moccasins

or the thirty different species of rattlesnake
or the tortoises, salamanders, centipedes, toads . . .

It takes some doing, all that,
but Ham comes back with them.
And wouldn't you know,
it's Japheth who opens up, so to speak,
the can of worms. "Dad, there are thousands
of species of worms! Who's
going digging for them? And oh, yes,
how about the insects?"
"Insects!" Shem rebels at last,
"Dad, do we have to save *insects?*" Noah,
faithful servant, quotes the Word:
"Every living thing."
"But Dad, the cockroaches?"
Noah has all the best instincts
of a minor bureaucrat—he
is only following orders—the roaches
go aboard.

Japheth ticks away at his roster. "So far
we've got dragonflies, damselflies, locusts, and aphids,
grasshoppers, mantises, crickets, and termites . . .
Wait a minute—termites?
We're going to save termites, in a wooden boat?"
But Japheth knows that arguing with Noah
is like driving a nail into chicken soup. He shrugs
and carries on. "We've got lice,
beetles—God knows how many beetles.

We've got bedbugs, cooties, gnats, and midges,
horseflies, sawflies, bottleflies, fireflies.
We've got ants, bees, wasps, hornets—
can you imagine what it's going to be like
cooped up with *them* for a whole year?
But Dad, we haven't even scratched the surface.
There must be a million species
of insects out there.
Even if we unload all the other animals,
the insects alone will sink the ark!''

Ah, but the ark was not floating on fact,
it was floating on faith—that is to say,
on fiction. And in fiction, the insects
went aboard—*and* a year's supply
of hay for the elephants, a year's bananas
for the monkeys, and so on.
"Well, that's that," Japheth says,
"but you still haven't answered my question—
what will the meat-eaters eat?"
"We'll cross that bridge when we come to it,"
Noah replies, in history's
least appropriate trope.
"All aboard, now, it's starting
to sprinkle."

So the fountains of the great deep
were broken up, and the windows of heaven opened,
and the rain was upon the earth
forty days and forty nights,

and the ark was lifted up
and went upon the face of the waters—
and the drowning began.
Noah pretended not to know,
and so did Shem and Ham, so
it was only Japheth who keened
for Enos and Jared, still out there
somewhere, and for Adah and beautiful Zillah.
He was the first to peek
out of the one small window, and yes,
there it was, just the way fear
had been painting it on his eyelids ever since
that divine command: people fighting
for high ground, crazed beasts goring
and gnashing, serpents dangling from trees.
Finally, Shem, Ham, and Noah
and the four nameless wives
couldn't resist—they looked out the window, too,
and watched their friends
hugging in love and panic until
they all went under. Japheth caught
one final glimpse, and of course it had to be Zillah,
holding her baby over her head
till the water rolled over her
and she sank, and the baby
splashed a little, and then
there was silence upon the waters,
and God was well pleased.
They all turned away from the window, Noah
and his sons and the weeping women,

and no one would look into anyone's eyes
for many days.

Twelve hard months that strange menagerie lived
in the ark, the sixteen thousand hungry birds
lusting for the two million insects,
and the twelve thousand snakes and lizards
nipping at the seven thousand mammals,
and everyone slipping and sliding around
on the sixty-four thousand worms
and the one hundred thousand spiders—
and Noah driving everyone buggy, repeating
every morning, as if he'd just thought of it,
"Well, we're all in the same boat."
It was a long, long year
for those weary men and their bedraggled wives,
feeding the gerbils and hamsters, cleaning
the thousands of cages, keeping the jaguars
away from the gazelles, the grizzlies away
from the cottontails—everything aboard, after all,
was an endangered species.
But finally the waters subsided,
the dove fluttered off and never returned,
the gangplank slid down to Ararat,
and the animals scrambled out to the muddy,
corpse-ridden earth.

And Noah, burning a lamb on his altar
under that mocking rainbow, cannot forget
that he rescued the snakes and spiders, but

he let Enoch and Jubal
and Cainan and Lamech and
their wives and innocent children
go to a soggy grave.
And Noah knows, in his tired bones,
that now he will have to be fruitful once more,
and multiply, and replenish the earth
with a pure new race of people who
would never, never sin again,
for if they did,
all that killing would be for nothing,
a terrible embarrassment
to God.

WATCHING HER SLEEP ~

On her left side, her right arm pillowed,
the breathing regular as waves:
it's summertime, and childhood,
her father come to life
to smooth her hair and stroll the grassy
sidewalk toward the sundaes at Prince Castle.
Coming home alone she flies
inches off the ground and finds her mother
saying go to sleep—it almost wakes her—
a quarter turn, worry in the forehead,
then the steady breathing.
No one thinks it odd she's outdoors
naked—once again
the streets are full of dimes.
But when our early neighbor
starts the mower, she
can't see where she's going
in the dark, something huge
chases her along a stone wall,
falling, falling . . .
She fights for breath,
flops over, blinks at daylight.
The warmth of arms is my reward
for the gallantry of simply
being there.

ANOTHER WORD FOR JIM

(James Wright, 1927–1980)

In the Middlewest, where dusty cornfields
whisper their earthy secrets, and
on the banks of the river Drim, outnumbered
five to one by the thundering Russians
casting their poems like stones,
we drank the white lightning of the pure
clear word—trees
like slender bodies,
horses in love with spring. Now
the rest of us are aging, but you
are out there again in the pastureland,
your music in all the timeless places:
in the slender trees,
in whispering cornfields, deep
in the desperate heart.

LIFE ON THE MISSISSIPPI QUEEN ⁓

> *It is easier to manufacture seven facts*
> *than one emotion.*
>
> —Mark Twain

The numbing plunge of the mud,
gorging and guzzling, force-
feeding the mouth of it, all
ravening down to the gulf,
billions of bushels and barrels,
hundred-weights, hoppers, and holds, no
starveling passions here, only the burden
of much, and more, draft
and ballast, deadweight tonnage,
love and hate and anger baffled,
no exaltation, no
epiphanies come of this, only
the crushing pressure, bite and chew
and swallow, the future drowning in
on stuff, and stuff, and stuff.

FLEAS

I form the light, and create darkness:
I make peace, and create evil:
I the Lord do all these things.
—Isaiah 45:7

I think that I shall never see
a poem as ugly as a flea,
a flea whose hungry mouth is pressed
against a buttock or a breast,
a flea that spreads disease all day
and lifts its little claws to prey:
poems are made by you and me,
but only God can make a flea.

I think that no one ever made
a poem as powerful as AIDS,
or plagues that may in summer kill
half the bishops in Brazil
and share the good Lord's Final Answer
with clots and cholera and cancer—
for God concocted pox to mock us,
staph and syph and streptococcus:
poems are made by bards or hacks,
but only God makes cardiacs.

I think that I shall never smell
a poem as pungent as a hell,
where grinning devils turn the screws
on saintly Sikhs and upright Jews,

giving them the holy scorcher,
timeless, transcendental torture:
poems can make you want to yell,
but only God can give you hell.

JONAH ◞

You remember the old story,
a fisherman bragging about the one
that got away: "This big," he says,
"this big it was, you never saw such a fish."
"No," says the other guy, "and neither did you."
It was that kind of day—on the run
from God, I stowed away
on the S.S. *Tarshish,* got
dry-heave sick in a wicked wind,
dreaded for hours the creaky tub
would sink the lot of us, finally
got flung overboard by panicky sailors
like so much ballast, and then,
after all that, to see this monster
come bearing down on me like I was
breakfast—oh,
you can see why I've been a little fuzzy
ever since. Was I really inside—
like people are saying now—I mean
really inside that fish, or whale,
or whatever it was, every eyewitness
gives you a different story—anyway,
was I *really*
in the belly of that thing
for three whole days?

I know what you're thinking—
"If *you* don't know, who does?" That's
what you're thinking, isn't it? Well,
don't get smug, this

is stickier than you think.
You've had those days, don't tell me you haven't—
you brush the cobwebs out of your eyes,
cursing the sunrise,
and there's that big jug
sitting there empty, and you say, my God,
did I drink it all? And the truth is,
you don't remember. It's like that.
I do remember this big mouth coming at me
like a tidal wave, and the next thing I know
it's three days later, and I'm on the beach,
hungry as a seagull and ready to kill
for a mug of the good stuff. But
what exactly had happened?

I know there's this rumor going around
that I was inside that fish, but wait
a minute, look at my skin—
all in one piece. How
could I have been swallowed and not been
chewed up, or at least munched on a little? Or
suppose I did somehow get gulped down whole,
and didn't break my neck going through
that churning gullet, then
what did I do for air for three days,
down there with all those squid and dead herring?
Just try to picture that scene,
as I do all the time now—
swimming in belly-soup, seasick whenever
the beast does its foraging dance,
and when it cranks up its digestive machine,

the squid and I get sprayed
with acid strong enough
to eat away my sandals.
And maybe the whale, or whatever it was,
gets lucky, hits a school
of irresistible tidbits,
and all of a sudden I'm dumped on by a ton
of fresh mackerel.
Am I supposed to believe
I survived all that for three days
and three nights, the gristly stomach
grinding away at everything inside,
squeezing me to mush? Oh,
come on!

Look, if you're so crazy
about the fish story, I've got a lot
of others you'd like—maybe
the one where Moses' staff turns into a snake,
or the time he splits the Red Sea like an apple,
or when Joshua knocks down a stone wall
by yelling at it,
or when Samson kills a thousand armed men
with a piece of bone—say,
I could go on and on. And if
you swear to me you swallow all that,
I mean really absolutely believe it
at high noon on a sunny summer day,
then maybe I'll think again about
swallowing the whale.

GIFTS ～

A winter birthday:
deep freeze out of the Yukon,
a battery dead as a dinosaur,
and an icy *Times,* its everyday smudge
full of the world as usual—famine,
murder, nukes, and the government still busy
taking bread from poets to feed the generals.
I'm finding it hard to remember when
life was a three-ring circus, all August
and sunshine and cotton candy. I do remember
that on my eighth birthday I wrote a poem
rhyming snowman and popcorn and clown,
and that very summer I saw my first circus:
poetry makes things happen.
The birds and the beasts were there, lions
in yellow cages, like animal crackers,
elephants doing their soft-shoe, and
in that magic circle,
monkeys riding clowns riding horses.
When they picked out kids
to join the parade, I found myself
grasping a mane, and flying—and afterward
two sequined beauties kissed my cheeks,
painting me up like a symbol. No wonder, then,
juggling a lifetime, I
felt the frost at midnight,
watched the woods fill up with snow,
and as the windchill dropped
to twenty below this morning,
warmed my hands at the darling buds of May,
at mermaids singing each to each,

at a magic circle where there are
no nukes or famines or tricky politicians,
but troubadours in motley doing cartwheels,
and bards on unicycles testing the high wire,
and minstrels in cap and bells taming the lions, brave
high-flying poets, all my sisters
and brothers, ready to blow out their candles
and make the same wish again, nothing extravagant,
only,
in their sponge rubber noses and polka dots,
to sing forever.

BEFORE YOU PUSH THE RED BUTTON ⁓

You need to know what it is,
what it really is that you're doing, so
there are certain requirements.

One: take a razor blade and make a slit
through your fingernail, from the cuticle
out to the edge; then two more slits, one
on each side.

Two: pick up the pliers and grip firmly
one of the strips of fingernail
and pull it off, all the way off,
allowing for the extra resistance
at the root. Do the same
to the other three strips, then proceed
to the next nail. It may not be easy at first,
but be firm. Pushing the red button, after all,
isn't kid stuff.

Three: when that hand is finished, do the other.
You'll notice that you never really
get used to the fine
texture of ripping flesh, so
take a ten-minute break, then

Four: do the toes. At last
you're beginning to understand
the red button; you have some pale
impression of a winter
of mutilations, a desert of epitaphs.
One more thing:

for anyone with a red button
who happens to be a slow learner,
there are other requirements, involving
Five / Six / Seven: the tongue / the eyeballs /
the genitals.

III

THE TREE OF
KNOWLEDGE

AND THEN THE PERFECT TRUTH OF HATRED

There was a preacher in our town
whose Sunday text was the Prince of Peace,
but
when he looked out at the Monday world—
at the uppity blacks and pushy Jews
and sassy wives and sneaky heathen—blood
scalded his face as purple as if
he'd hung by his heels. Then
his back-yard, barber-shop, street-corner sermons
scorched us with all the omens of siege:
our roofs aflame, tigers at the gates,
hoodlums pillaging homes, ravaging
wives and daughters, the sky
come crashing down,
and we gazed into his blazing truth
of Onward Christian Soldiers,
A Mighty Fortress Is Our God,
Soldiers of the Cross. No question now
of sissy charity, this
was the Church Militant, burning
its lightning bolts across
our low horizons.

It's been a while since that preacher went off
to the big apartheid in the sky,
and the only hint of eternal life
is the way he resurrects each week
to sell salvation on the screen.
He's younger after all these years,
in designer suits and toothy smiles,
but we know him by the cunning eyes

where he harbors his old stooges,
Satan, Jehovah. He calls them up,
and across the country, glands begin
pumping bile into our lives:
sleet storms in the voice,
cords in the neck like bullwhips,
broken promises, broken bones—
the wreckage of his deep
sincerity.

MARY 〜

Years later, it was, after everything
got hazy in my head—those buzzing flies,
the gossips, graybeards, hustling evangelists—
they wanted facts, they said,
but what they were really after
was miracles.
Miracles, imagine! I was only a girl
when it happened, Joseph
acting edgy and claiming
it wasn't his baby . . .

Anyway, years later
they wanted miracles, like the big-time cults
up in Rome and Athens, God
come down in a shower of coins,
a sexy swan, something like that.
But no, there was only
one wild-eyed man at our kitchen window
telling me I'm lucky.
And pregnant.
I said, "Talk sense, mister, it's got to be
the one thing or the other."
No big swans, no golden coins
in that grubby mule-and-donkey village. Still,
they wanted miracles,
and what could I tell them? He
was my baby, after all, I washed
his little bum, was I
supposed to think I was wiping
God Almighty?

But they *wanted miracles,* kept after me
to come up with one: "This fellow at the window,
did he by any chance have wings?"
"Wings! Do frogs have wings?
Do camels fly?"
They thought it over. "Cherubim," they said,
"may walk the earth like men
and work their wonders."
I laughed in their hairy faces. No
cherub, that guy! But
they wouldn't quit—fanatics, like
the gang *he* fell in with years ago,
all goading him till he began to believe
in quick cures and faith-healing,
just like the cranks in Jerusalem, every
phony in town speaking in tongues
and handling snakes. Not exactly
what you'd want for your son, is it?
I tried to warn him, but he just says,
"I must be about my father's business."
"Fine," I say, "I'll buy you a new
hammer." But nothing could stop him, already
hooked on the crowds, the hosannas,
the thrill of needling the bureaucrats.
Holier than thou, he got, roughing up
the rabbis even. Every night
I cried myself to sleep—my son,
my baby boy . . .

You know how it all turned out, the crunch
of those awful spikes,

the spear in his side, the whole town watching,
home-town folks come down from Nazareth
with a strange gleam in their eyes. Then later on
the grave robbers, the hucksters, the imposters all
claiming to be him. I was sick
for a year, his bloody image
blurring the sunlight.

And now they want miracles, God
at my maidenhead, sex without sin.
"Go home," I tell them, "back to your libraries,
read about your fancy Greeks,
and come up with something amazing, if you must."

Me, I'm just a small-town woman,
a carpenter's wife, Jewish mother, nothing
special. But listen,
whenever I told my baby a fairy tale,
I let him know it was a fairy tale.
Go, all of you, and do likewise.

CREDO 〜

I am modern. And educated. And reasonable.
And I believe in Jesus Christ, son
of the living God.
When they tell me He
was born of a virgin, I say, well,
it's unusual, of course, but in the arms of God,
anything is possible . . .
When they tell me that a bright new star
appeared in the eastern sky,
shining over His manger, I say, well,
I know it's not customary
to improvise stars like that, but remember,
we set up searchlights now, just
to open a used-car lot, and after all,
this *is* the Son of God, isn't it? . . .
They tell me He cast out demons,
and I say, well,
you have to understand the peculiar idiom
of a given historical time . . .
They tell me His voice could calm a tempest,
and I reflect on all the unexplained
phenomena
of our physical world . . .
They tell me His touch cured blindness,
made the lame walk, the lepers clean,
and brought corpses back to life—
and I'm reminded of the psychic component
of so much modern medicine . . .
They tell me He fed five thousand
with five loaves and two fishes,
that He walked on the surface of the sea,

that He rose from the dead—
and I relish the poetic truth
of those venerable symbols.

In the backward villages of Asia,
the gods have as many limbs
as spiders, and take on monstrous forms
as quickly as a cloud. The natives,
shrouded in their age-old ignorance
and superstition, believe
the most bizarre tales about them,
despite the best efforts
of our enlightened missionaries.

COAST TO COAST ∼

The bird that shook the earth at J.F.K.
goes blind to milkweed, riverbanks, the wrecks
of elm trees full of liquor and decay—
and jars the earth again at L.A.X.

Once, on two-lane roads, our crazy drives
across the country tallied every mile
in graves or gardens: glimpses in our lives
to make the busy continent worthwhile.

Friendly, then, the smell of woods and fields,
the flash of finches and the scud of crows,
the rub of asphalt underneath our wheels
as tangible as sand between the toes.

From orchards out to prairies, then to cactus,
the rock and mud and clay were in our bones:
as birches turned to oak, then eucalyptus,
we learned our lover's body stone by stone.

Now, going home we're blind again, seven
miles above the earth on chartered wings:
in a pressurized and air-conditioned heaven
the open road's a song nobody sings.

JUDAS ⌇

Ask Peter, ask Paul—the really unbearable part
was figuring out those hillbilly parables.
We understood the straight stuff, "Blessed
are the peacemakers," and such, but not
those constant "It is like unto's . . ."
They always sent shivers through us—we knew
there'd be catechism after the sermon.
"It is like unto sowing seeds," he'd say
in that Nazarene country drawl,
"some of them fall on good soil,
others on rock." Well, everybody knows that,
but what did he mean by it?
He'd only say, "Who hath ears to hear,
let him hear." Big help.
Or he'd say, "It is like unto a mustard seed
that grows into a huge plant." Mmm-hmm.
He'd say, "The kingdom of heaven
is like unto leaven," and so on.
And then, of course, that inevitable
"Who hath ears to hear," etcetera.
We were always as nervous as cats in a doghouse,
John sneaking glances at James, James
dragging his toe in the sand and looking
at Thomas, Thomas looking doubtful,
all of us hoping that someone would understand.
But we never did, not one single time—finally
he always had to explain. "The *field*
is the *world,*" he'd say, his eyebrows grim
as a tax collector, "The good seed
are the children of the kingdom, get it?"
Oh, sure, it's easy when you already

know the answer, but
suppose it'd been you, hearing
for the hundredth time
those words like needles in your nerves,
"It is like unto, it is like unto . . ."
It drives you over the edge, finally, even
Peter claiming he didn't know him,
and I . . . Well,
with or without those thirty pieces of silver,
it's a wonder that none of the others
crossed him first.

THIN ICE

Just at the brittle edge of love,
where life can snap off at a touch,
we glide along, testing
our toughness. It holds.
We circle back and try it again
and again, each time more daring
by the space of a thrill,
a sliding of fear and fever, knowing
that ice can melt as well as break.
So we take our chances,
holding our breath,
trying for something no one
has ever done.

HEADING NORTH ～

Day breaks
your heart: pack
the smell of tanning oil
beside your snorkels and
whip your bones to a raw
future, dragging along
the pain of orchids and
hibiscus. Home again,
fighting your way through slush,
you are condemned to memories
of angelfish in coral reefs,
dazzling your frosted eyeballs. Now
your slurred footsteps
won't beat the walk light; nothing
the color of palm trees blossoms
on Tenth Street. Wake, if you must,
to half-hour delays
in the morning rush, prophecies
of turmoil in the sky,
minutes carefully pieced together
for the sake of a thousand nothings. But
dream, in your bickering taxis,
of the slow wake of white sails,
your purest vision turning in
upon itself, leaving
everything to chance except
your life:
the sun on your pale back,
the lust of ocean along your skin,
a lifetime that's finally worth it
every time you breathe.

MARTHA ～

(Martha Haberkorn, 1899–1983)

Planting trees, ironing shirts,
visiting shut-ins: imagine her
moving from sink to stove,
from need to need,
and on Sundays glittering
with stained glass, hearing always
the praises of a jealous God,
and every night His fierce voice
hissing, "Listen, listen,
   a fire is kindled in mine anger
   and shall burn unto the lowest hell,
   and sinners shall be devoured
   with burning heat and with bitter destruction,
   the teeth of beasts, the poison of serpents,
   the sword without, and terror within,
   to Me belongeth vengeance."
Thus
spake the Lord.

So when the bad times came to her troubled mind
and she bore the modern torture of her pills
and the ancient menace of the lakes of fire,
and every night came on in a black torment,
then the Lord was faithful to her bed,
reminding her in the dangerous hours
of all the evil things she'd ever done—
the omissions, the white lies, the private
secrets locked away—little
derelictions from

her eighty-four years of goodness.
And God would not relent
when her body trembled
and her words came in gargling
whispers—when, in the dark chambers
of the heart, the pounding
was hammers on nerve-ends—the sword without,
the terror within—and a tiny voice
grieved her guilty life:
"I've done so many bad things, and now
Jesus won't forgive me, the Lord
won't let me rest."

How can we then forgive this God
who will not forgive His saints?
We are here to witness
that the sins of the Lord are past pardon.
He is therefore banished from our planet
to shuffle through a universe of stars,
while the tree of knowledge sows its golden apples
all across this land.

LIGHTING YOUR BIRTHDAY CAKE ∼

Of course we didn't come this far
without leaving a trail, but it's only
footprints on a beach: one wash
through our memories, and it's gone. Strange,
so much passion, commitment, doomed
to be drifted over like
Troy and Babylon, pitiful echoes now
of all those eager heartbeats.
You've always cared so much,
about us, sure, but really everything—
hungry kids, dolphins, over-
population, and the old foes: batterers, bishops,
gunslingers, chauvinists—nothing escapes
your rage or compassion; earthquakes in Asia
shake our midnight bedroom. You always knew
that the bright bird of sympathy
is the only godliness on earth,
hovering over these grubby streets
on better wings than angels'. Now
I can't believe in a world without
your bonfire of outrage, small flame of anguish,
pink glow of happiness.
Remember how I need your warmth:
as you blow out these candles, make a wish
to keep the fires burning.

JESUS 〜

We're cast in the image of God,
they say, but
up here the image blurs—
that Pharisee at the edge of the crowd,
the one with a burro's belly
and a toad's complexion—
is he the real thing, God
in the flesh?
Or maybe that saintly starveling, all
bones in her pinched piety—does God
have a profile like hers?

Just days ago, these very faces,
rainbowed with joy, saw palm trees
ripped and strewn for the son of man. Now
my palms are red,
and it's all changed—bloodlust
smudges the thousand grins
of God. Here
in this Friday frenzy, just
look at them, the veins
in that legionnaire's legs, the brutal
mouth, the pocked face, and . . .
And of course the handsome boy out there
eyeing the splendid line
of that girl's arm—them, too.
It all counts,
doesn't it?

I suppose they aren't even wondering,
this godly rabble out for fun,

expecting something big today, something
spectacular. So I should be telling them,
now, before I'm dust forever—
you don't pay off an ugly squint
with a nice ankle; a luscious
lower lip doesn't make up
for a running sore; and above all, nobody
ever promised you justice.
All you have to know is
that a beautiful shoulder is God, but
a twisted leg is God, too,
and crooked noses and bad teeth. This
is the real revelation—that God
is only a trick with mirrors, our
dark reflection in a glass.

So up here, getting this panoramic view,
I hear the voices of God on every side,
all mocking me, "Hold on,
it's your big scene!" And I cry out
to every smooth and sacred cheek,
to every holy wart and pustule—the spikes
tearing at my hands—I call to every
body on this hill of skulls,
Why?
Why have you
forsaken me?

BUT THE DAISIES WILL NOT BE ～
DECEIVED BY THE GODS

Seductions as countless as crosses,
as icons, none of it ever
surprising, not even
the stare of the sky
keeping score. The prize for yielding,
for giving in to paradise,
is laying down the awful burden
of mind: surrender
rings from the steeples and calls
from the minarets and temples.
But challenges sing
in the sway of treetops,
in the flutter of sparrows,
in chirring and stalking,
in waking and ripening—let
there be light enough, and
everywhere backbone stiffens
in saplings and clover. Praises, then,
to sunfish and squirrels,
blessings to bugs. Turning our backs
on the bloody altars,
we cherish each other, living here
in this brave world
with our neighbors, the earthworms,
and our old friends, the ferns
and the daisies.